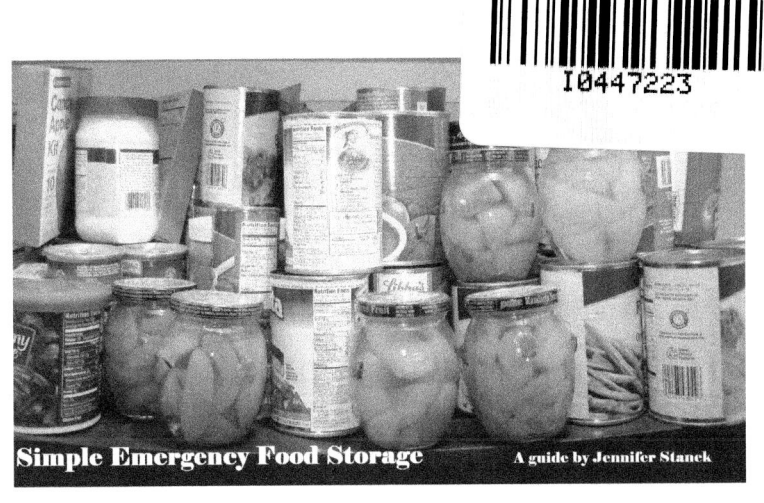

Simple Emergency Food Storage — A guide by Jennifer Stanek

Simple

Emergency Food Storage

PUBLISHED BY:
Jennifer Stanek
Copyright © 2012

Table of contents

Introduction-

Keeping and Emergency food Storage Supply is essential to your family's security in uncertain times. It can save your life and your loved ones lives when disaster strikes. Be prepared, be self-reliant, and secure in knowing you won't starve in an emergency with this helpful guide. I have made this book as short as possible, yet it contains all the information needed to get the job done, without all the bloat and filler other books contain.

I have included pictures of the steps involved and items needed. By the time you are finished reading this straight forward, simple book, you will have all the knowledge required to start you on your way to a realistic Emergency Food Storage plan. The side benefit is that you can make your food costs practically non-existent while living on a small budget.

Emergency food supplies are critical to your family's well-being and security in today's economy, as well as protection from natural disasters.

Sudden circumstances can leave you and your family without food and water in a matter of days if you go grocery shopping once a week, or every couple of days. Fresh food only stays fresh for a week at best in the refrigerator, and that is only if the power is on! Frozen food seems like a good idea, but they are only good for 24 hours after the power goes out. Not to mention the bad economy, what would you do if you lost your job? How would you provide food for yourself and family without money?

Section- 1 Anything is possible

Are you are concerned about surviving a temporary situation or a natural disaster?

Maybe you are worried about 2012 or you just want extra food on hand to save trips to the grocery store; storing freeze-dried and canned food can give you peace of mind on a daily basis.

No more worrying about what to eat, where to go to get free handouts, and not to mention the ability to have all kinds of great foods available when you run out in the kitchen. Having an emergency food storage can save you last-minute trips to the store.

Think about the following:

There are natural disasters happening around the world today that still have not been supplied with the bare necessities to live. People die from not getting food and water, the government only has so much to pass out, not to mention if they can get to you. You must insure your own life, do not trust anyone with your life. Only you can save yourself.

Keeping emergency food storage will keep you out of the crowds that fight for a bag of rice and the various dangers of scavengers that prey on people that can't defend themselves. Look at the hurricanes on the east coast of the USA and Gulf of Mexico, there are still homeless hungry people there that the government hasn't gotten to yet, if ever. You can ensure you will at least be able to eat if you need to leave your home, or can't leave. Leaving the safety of your home will not be an issue whether you stay or need to leave; you WILL have food to eat until help comes or to take on the road to get to safety.

Tsunamis are a big concern on the coastal regions as well, most recently Japan. There are entire towns washed away, people walking around with nothing. If they had at least a BOB (bug out bag)-back pack with at least 2 days food and water, they could have made it to safety. Food and water are essential in an emergency. If the cost of gas continues to rise, your food prices rise as well. Trucks and trains deliver your food to your area and if those systems get expensive or fail you must be prepared.

The reality of your dependence on other people to provide you with food is not to be taken lightly. Think of starting emergency food storage as insurance, real life insurance. Only you can save yourself.

Section- 2   Making space

Setting up an area for your food storage is easy. It doesn't have to be an entire room, of half of the basement or garage. Keeping your emergency food stored in a dry, dark, cool place is essential. I have used a closet that just had junk in it I didn't need.

Clear or colored plastic totes are great to keep your supplies in. Dry goods, wet, canned, and freeze-dried items will be protected from floods and light. A plastic shelving unit to organize your totes inside a closet is what I have found to be the best solution. Make sure to measure the closet door and the shelving unit, so it will fit inside. If you can assemble it inside the closet then make sure there is plenty of room.

Decide on how much food you will need or want to keep on hand. A week's worth of food for each member of the family is a good idea, however much you feel comfortable with is best to start. Something is better than nothing, so begin small and build your supplies up over time.

The only requirement for a place to store your emergency food supply is that it must be cool, below 70 F, and out of direct sunlight. Under the bed is an option, a kitchen pantry, anywhere you have space available that is easily accessible in an emergency.

Those are the basics when looking at your home or apartment deciding on where to put your food. Remember not to place your emergency food storage next to a furnace, hot water heater, stove, wall heater, water lines, or electrical panels. Keep a common sense approach to deciding on where to store your food. If you have a lot of guests in your home or want to keep it private that you have a food storage, which I recommend, don't use a space that can be seen by other people easily.

The food you have stored may save your life one day, and if other people know about it, they may try to take it from you when disaster strikes the town, city, or community. This may sound absurd, however when 99% of people are placed in a survival situation they will become irrational, and they want to survive as well.

If anyone knows about your emergency food storage then the first place they will think of going is to your home! If it comes down to "you or them", wouldn't you rather have it be YOU who survives? YOU planned ahead. You prepared yourself for an emergency. You have the supplies to feed yourself and your family, no one else. If those supplies are used by another person will you have enough to survive? This is about your personal survival. Keep it private and protected.

Section- 3

Long term storage foods

Nutrition is an important factor to keep in mind when preparing an emergency food storage area. Keep at least one group of vegetables, meats, fruits, vitamins, and lots of water. If you have a good selection of foods that are high in vitamins and proteins, along with water and vitamins you will be able to survive a short time. The food pyramid is a great guide to follow, but for survival; just the basics are necessary.

Most of the guides or books out there focus on organic foods, and healthy options, which I definitely encourage you to eat on a daily basis. Your health is #1, however when in a survival situation the last thing you are considering is if the food you have stored is organic. In fact the more preservatives the better! That's right, I am saying it! Now if you are planning on using your emergency food supply as a supplement to your regular food consumption, go with the healthier option.

If you have the money, and commit to starting with ALL organic options then you must decide now, and replenish the items you consume as soon as possible.

As you know the organic foods do not store as long, and can contaminate the other items in your storage if they leak, or rot. You want your emergency food storage to last as long as possible, so it will be ready long after you have invested in it, therefore an organic choice is not the best, but it is a personal preference.

Types of long term storage foods

-<u>Canned food</u> is the easiest to buy, and there is such a variety that you can just buy and store canned food to start. Some canned food does not keep for more than a year, so be careful what you buy, get the longest time from purchase expiration date possible. The drawback to canned food is the weight, and amount of space they take up. I have about 50% of my supply as canned goods that are used on a regular basis to keep them fresh

-<u>Freeze-dried foods</u> will keep up to 25 years if kept in a cool dark place. They taste good too, and come in every single variety that you can think of, from vegetable, to meat, even bacon. Freeze dried fruit is very good, and don't forget about milk and butter. Just add water and they are exactly the same as what's in your fridge. I have found they are the best option for long term storage, especially if you are looking for food security.

-<u>MRE</u> (meals ready to eat) are a very good choice as well, I have never had a bad tasting one. I take them camping, hiking, and fishing. The advantage of MRE's is that no water is required to hydrate them.

MRE's taste just like the real thing, because they are the real thing. I have had really good tasting MRE's that I can't believe aren't prepared fresh. The storage life varies for MRE's, from 3 years 10 15 on average, I have personally eaten one 12 years old, and it lost some flavor, but was perfectly fine.

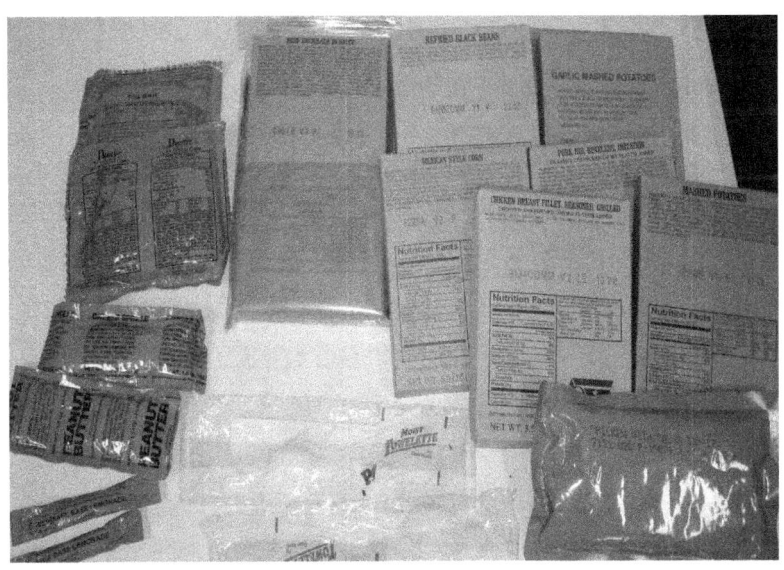

-<u>Bulk dry food</u> items are very easy to store, have a very long shelf life, and always come out the way you want them to when cooked. Large bags of rice, granola, flour, sugar, and salt are the best options available to start with. Sugar is self storing, which means you don't have to worry about it going bad as long as it is in a sealed container.

-<u>Noodles</u> are great to store since they can be used easily and don't go bad in a sealed bag or container. Noodles last a very long time as sugar does, just be sure to keep them in an air-tight container.

-<u>Honey</u> is the absolute best item for long term storage as it never goes bad! Honey has been found in Egyptian tombs still edible! It can be used in so many ways that it is a must for your emergency food storage. It needs no special storage requirements, no cooking, or any special care other than keep it in a sealed container. Honey can be used on wounds as a topical anti-biotic to fight infections as well as the nutritional value.

-<u>Peanut butter</u> is a great addition to your long term storage as well. It has high protein content and high on calories. It can be stored for a year or 3 at best, however it will separate from the oils that it is mixed with to give it a creamy texture, just stir after opening.

You can also purchase cereals, dry drink mixes, and beans. The only way I store these items is by first vacuum sealing them with a home vacuum sealer. I purchased one from a big-box store and it has come in very handy for breaking up bulk items into smaller packages that are air tight. You can also use plastic baggies that have a press seal or tape them shut. Just be sure to date all of your stored items.

Keeping items that you regularly run out of in a storage place helps save gas and lost time when you are in the middle of cooking. Spices, salt, sugar, flour, tuna fish, and spaghetti noodles are some examples. Label the totes and packages with the date, and expiration date with a black permanent marker facing outwards so you can see the markings. This is so you know when it was packed and when to inspect them.

Whenever you package yourself, make sure to wash the area you are working in. Clean the counter or table with disinfectant, such as Lysol spray or bathroom cleaner. A teaspoon of bleach in about 3 gallons of water works great too. You do not want any bacteria in your food storage, which would be a waste of time and money. I always wear a pair of rubber surgical gloves, or dishwashing gloves that I disinfect prior to packaging anything. Keep everything clean and organized, it will make it so much easier for you to find when you need it also.

The one thing that will keep your emergency food supply fresh and protected from going bad for a long time are Oxygen Absorbers.

They absorb oxygen in the container with the food, preventing spoilage. You see these packed in vitamin bottles, beef jerky, and lots of pre-packaged foods you buy at the grocery store.

I put them in every single container that I package myself. They can be purchased online in bulk packs and they are very cheap. Search the internet and buy the best rated by other people, since quality can be varied even among the same manufacturer.

The following pages are pictures of a proper vacuum sealing/bagging set up:

#1 Clean the preparation surface, inside of the plastic tote and wash your hands before beginning.

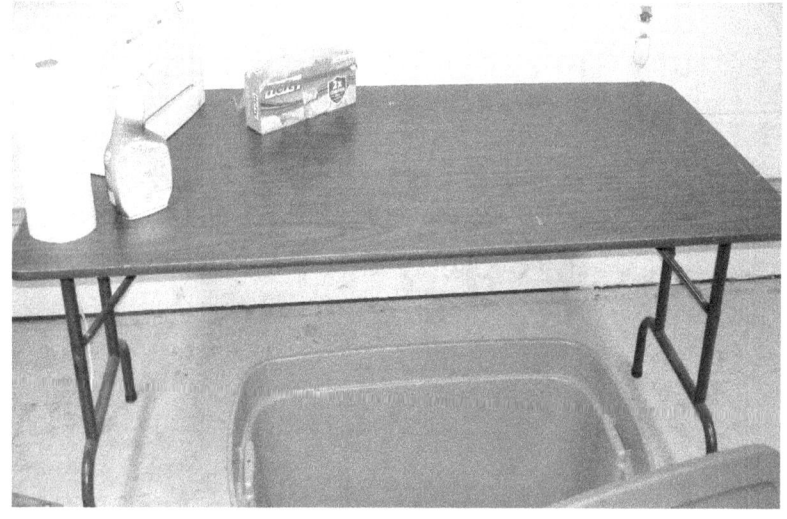

Here is a sanitized table, and tote ready to begin vacuum sealing or bagging items.

#2 Place the items you wish to package on the table, and get a black permanent marker handy to date items.

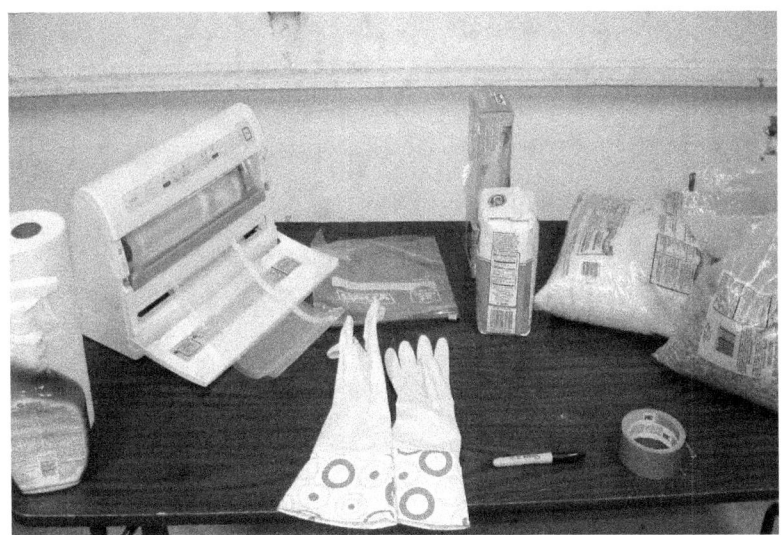

#3 Package and Date your foods and place them in your plastic totes.

Here is everything packaged, and dated. You will notice the blue oxygen absorbers in the bags.

Here is a closer picture of oxygen absorbers-

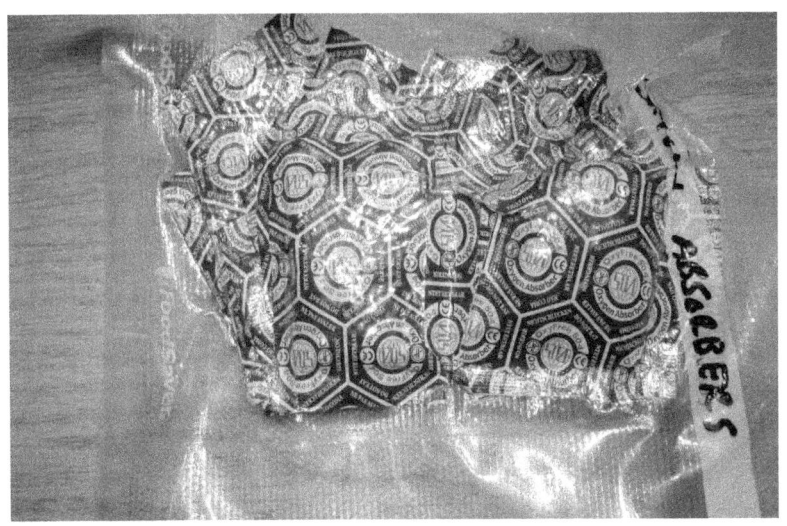

The oxygen absorbers are essential when re-packaging your bulk food; they will keep the food dry and prevent spoilage.

#4 Seal the tote with tape and place it in the storage area you have chosen.

A list of long term storage items-

1. Canned food

2. Freeze dried foods, mostly found cheapest online

3. MRE (meals ready to eat), can be found online for a mid to high price

4. Bulk dry goods purchased from the grocery store such as-

    A. Rice

    B. Granola

    C. Flour

    D. Sugar

    E. Salt

    F. Noodles (dry)

    G. Beans

    H. Dry drink mix

    I. Cereals (repackaged with vacuum sealer)

5. Spices

6. Tuna fish

7. Honey

8. Peanut butter

7. Oxygen absorbers (found cheap online)

8. Plastic bags or vacuum sealer set-up.

9. Tape to seal your totes.

Section- 4 Protecting your investment

The most important thing to do immediately after setting up your supply space is to protect it from the elements, especially rodents and insects. A plastic tote is great for keeping out insects and moisture if the lid seals tight, if not you can tape it shut.

For a closet or other room in the house you use to store your investment, keep the tote off the ground by placing it on top of some old pieces of wood or anything that supports the weight of the container. Rodents can be a problem if you improperly store your emergency food.

By far the one thing mice and rats can get into easily are plastic containers. They can smell everything inside that you carefully packed and chew right through it. The only thing I have found to work if you can stand the smell are mothballs, the Naphtha kind, not the newer ones.

Check the active ingredients on the box of mothballs, it should say- Naphtha. An alternative that I have found to work somewhat is mint oil, mice don't like it either. You can also set mouse and ant traps in the area surrounding your supplies, just remember to check them at least once a week.

If you keep the area around and near your supplies clean and in a closed room the likely hood of this happening is small. However just to be safe I recommend following these guidelines.

In summary-

1. In and around your storage area must be kept clean.
2. Seal your plastic tote with tape, preferably masking or packaging tape.
3. Keep your food raised off the ground as best as you can.
4. Use moth balls or mint oil to deter mice and insects.
5. Use mouse traps and ant traps to catch any animals that get in the area.
6. A closed room is the best place, in the dark and kept cold (below 70 F).

Section- 5 Rotate Stock

Remember to rotate your stock, yearly at a minimum. There is nothing worse than finding out all your canned tuna has spoiled when you need it.

Put all newly purchased items in the back of the storage area, and move the oldest to the front. Grocery stores do the same thing. When you buy milk you know what I mean. Looking for the milk with the latest dates can be hard when they bury the new milk in the back of the cooler.

Some foods go bad quicker than others, so keep that in mind when you create your storage area. A good rule of thumb is to put longer lasting foods on the right, and shorter life foods on the left. I have found this is easier to deal with when reaching for something I need in the kitchen to cook with. I won't grab something I intend to keep for an actual emergency, and I am not wasting my long term storage.

Remember:
First in first out!

Section- 6 Medication

Don't forget about prescription medication too. I always save a pill from each bottle I finish and store it for an emergency; you never know when those medications will be unavailable. Especially if you are diabetic! There are many herbal equivalents for prescription drugs, they will not replace them. They may get you by until you can get your prescribed medicine again.

A variety of medicinal teas should be kept on hand as well as homeopathic remedies, even if you think they don't work. The placebo effect may take affect when you don't have proper medication. Something is better than nothing. Any over the counter medication you can think of is a great idea, such as Tylenol, Aspirin, Neosporin, vitamins, etc...

Make a list here of any medications you are taking.

Section- 7 Bug out Bag (BOB)

A Bug out Bag or widely known as a BOB, can be a practical solution for those that don't have the space to set up a complete storage area, like in an apartment or rental unit. It is essentially a ready to go pack with all the things you will need if you need to leave your home in an emergency.

You can use an old backpack (best option), or luggage bag that is portable, and well made is recommended. Get together at least 1 day's worth of water (6 bottles conservatively) and food in the bag packed tightly.

The best option to have are MRE's, however some drink mix, beef jerky, and crackers are the easiest items to purchase for those that want to go the cheaper route. Your BOB will be an emergency medical kit as well for any injuries that may happen while getting to safety. You can buy first aid kits that are great, but plan on adding other items like a flashlight, and a small radio with plenty of batteries for both.

Don't forget a can opener or multi-tool that has a knife built in also, this can prove to be very useful when you least expect it. A good set of walkie-talkies is a good idea also to keep in contact with family members when you cannot see them close by. It is also a good idea to put a pair of pants, underwear, socks, and a shirt in the bag. That way if you get wet or contaminated you will have something to wear.

Put the clothing in a plastic bag, tied tightly in case it rains, then you will have dry clothes.

The final and last item I feel is necessary is *toilet paper*! Pack it as tight as possible in 2 or 3 rolls in a 1 gallon sealed plastic bag to keep it small and dry. Pack everything in as tight as you can. You are trying to survive until you can be rescued or find help so the smaller the better.

If you have room left, pack anything else you need for your mental health while you await rescue. A book or drawing materials, and small pocket games are great things to have while you rest.

Typical BOB contents-

1. 6 bottles of water, but as much as you can carry is best

2. Food (preferable MRE's), Beef jerky, crackers, canned tuna

   A- MRE's if in your budget (3 days supply)

   B. Beef jerky (1 bag)

   C. Crackers, whole wheat are the best option (about 50-100 individual)

   D. Canned foods that are lightweight, and not need re-hydrating, such as tuna (5 cans)

   E. Drink mix fortified with vitamins (about 15 single serve packs)

3. First-aid kit (small camping style one)

4. Flashlight with a set of spare batteries, or a solar/crank style

5. Multi-tool that has the essentials, knife, can opener, scissors, and tweezers

6. Full set of clothing, pants, shirt, socks, underwear, and a belt. (A ball cap can be great in hot weather also)

7. Walkie-talkies if there is more than just yourself in your household, and a spare set of batteries for each unit.

8. Toilet paper (2-3 rolls)

9. A cigarette lighter or water proof matches.

Section- 8 Water

The most important item in your food storage is *WATER*! Do not forget this item; it is the *cheapest*, and *most essential* to survival.

If you have freeze dried food, plan on having 2 times the amount you think you need or can store. Freeze dried food absorbs water to re-hydrate and can use up your supply of drinking water quickly. There are various places online to purchase water storage containers, or you can get a good water filter like a BigBerkey, or Katadyn.*

*links to purchase these filters are on my blog-
http://simpleemergencyfoodstorage.blogspot.com

With those two types of water filters you can drink any water you can scavenge, even very dirty muddy water. I recommend these two types in case your tap water gets contaminated.

A portable hand pump is useful if you have a source of water nearby as well. You can buy one that has a filter built in so you can save space and money. There are various prices for water filters but purchase one that is within your budget.

They are very useful to keep on hand when you run out of bottled water. The best is a portable. That way you can take it with you and not carry a 5 pound filter setup everywhere you go, making it clear you have or can get clean water to other survivors. Do not attract attention to yourself and keep your supplies to yourself; it is the best way to survive in a crowd of refugees.

If you run out of water, you chances of survival are very slim. You MUST have CLEAN water to survive for any amount of time! If you don't want to go that far into storage then keep 2-5 cases of bottled water in the house that is saved only for emergencies. If it expires you can still cook with it.

When storing water in a large container you should treat it. There are many different kinds of products to choose from. I will not go into how much is needed for each gallon etc... This information can be found online. I just use bottled water. It is easy, cheap, convenient, and lasts a long time without the need to handle chemicals. No need to complicate things more than necessary. This is supposed to be easy! Stick with bottled water to start, then if you feel the need and desire to get a large filter or water storage tank do some research on it. Bottled water is the best way I have found for the beginner.

Here are a couple of water storage options that are common with people that want to store large quantities of water:

 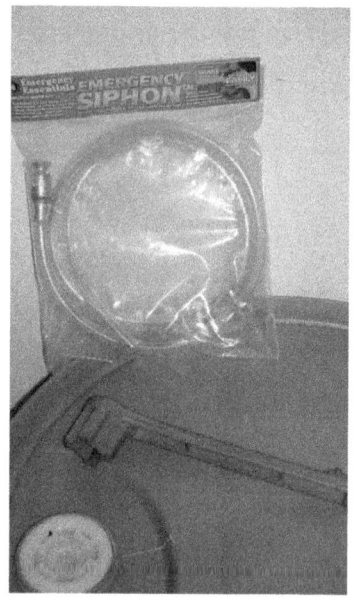

There is a 55 gallon and a 35 gallon water storage container, purchased from an online retailer. It is also a good idea to have a cap or bung tool to open and fill or drain the containers. also a siphon tube that will enable you to get water out of the container without setting it on its side.

There are MRE water packets as well that can be purchased separately from MRE sets. I would recommend this individual packaging since contamination will be limited to one package.

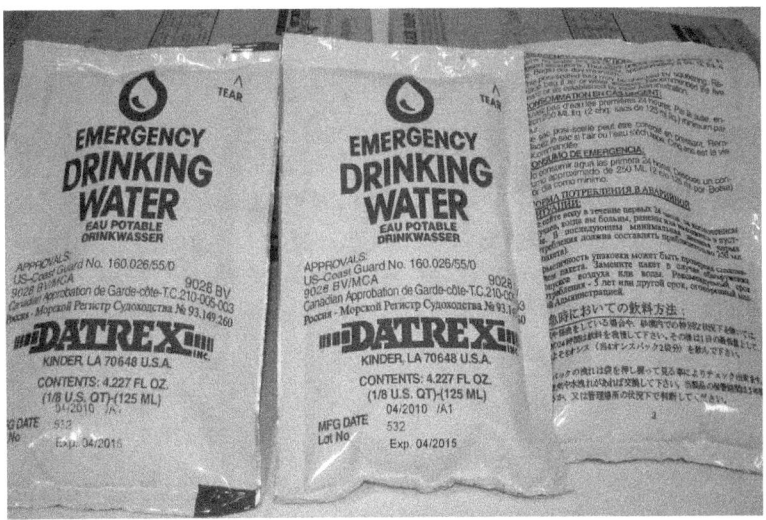

I use bottled water as my primary source of stored water. It is easy, cheap, and convenient. Not to mention it lasts a long time without the need to handle chemicals. No need to complicate things more than necessary. This is supposed to be easy! Stick with bottled water to start, then if you feel the need and desire to get a large filter or water storage tank do some research on it. Bottled water is the best way I have found for the beginner.

I recommend at least 3 cases (24 bottles per case) per person on hand in storage at a minimum, for a weeks' worth of water.

Section -9 3 Day Survival Storage Guidelines

The following is a list of items that I suggest should be kept for 3 days of emergency food survival for 1 person unable to leave the home. This is my recommended list of items that you can modify to your particular needs.

Remember to keep all the proper 5 food groups and lots of water, you can never have enough.

3 Days supplies for 1 person-

2 cases of bottled water
6 cans of potted meat or tuna fish
2 boxes of whole wheat crackers
1 jar of peanut butter
6 cans of vegetables of your choice
6 cans of fruit of your choice
3 cans of soup of your choice

Your BOB will also be essential if you need to leave your home, keep it in a safe and handy place.

This is a basic list; I did not include a lot of things. This is just to start off, add to it as you go along.

Your storage area can be stuffed full of everything and anything you want to store. As long as it has a long shelf life. If you can't leave your home, then this list will keep you alive. Store it in your plastic tote sealed and do not open it. Only open it for inspection once a year.

Conclusion

Keeping an emergency food supply will protect you from increasing food costs and give you an option when prices are so high you can only afford the basics. You will have vegetables when the crops are destroyed by bad weather and meat when there is none in the grocery stores. Even freeze dried milk and cheese when none exists in your area. Everything you need will be ready for you when the unexpected happens. You will have a chance to survive.

I hope this has enlightened you somewhat on the benefits of storing an Emergency Food Supply. Emergency food is a vital part of household security and personal survival in today's unpredictable economy. You can start small and have the peace of mind knowing you have everything you need in case of an emergency.

Simple and secure.

Check out my blog for updates and useful information, as well as links to purchase the items listed in this book-

http://simpleemergencyfoodstorage.blogspot.com

KEEP YOURSELF AND YOUR FAMILY SECURE, BEGIN AN EMERGENCY FOOD STORAGE TODAY!